SEASONAL GIFTS
& *festive*
celebrations

SEASONAL GIFTS
& festive
celebrations

recipes and ideas for handmade holiday gifts

SARAH AINLEY

southwater

This edition is published by Southwater

Southwater is an imprint of Anness Publishing Ltd
Hermes House, 88–89 Blackfriars Road, London SE1 8HA
tel. 020 7401 2077; fax 020 7633 9499
www.southwaterbooks.com; info@anness.com

© Anness Publishing Ltd 1997, 2003

UK agent: The Manning Partnership Ltd,
tel. 01225 478444; fax 01225 478440; sales@manning-partnership.co.uk

UK distributor: Grantham Book Services Ltd,
tel. 01476 541080; fax 01476 541061; orders@gbs.tbs-ltd.co.uk

North American agent/distributor: National Book Network,
tel. 301 459 3366; fax 301 429 5746; www.nbnbooks.com

Australian agent/distributor: Pan Macmillan Australia,
tel. 1300 135 113; fax 1300 135 103; customer.service@macmillan.com.au

New Zealand agent/distributor: David Bateman Ltd,
tel. (09) 415 7664; fax (09) 415 8892

All rights reserved. No part of this publication may be reproduced, stored in a retrieval
system, or transmitted in any way or by any means, electronic, mechanical, photocopying, recording or otherwise,
without the prior written permission of the copyright holder.

A CIP catalogue record for this book is available from the British Library.

Publisher: Joanna Lorenz
Copy Editor: Beverley Jollands
Designer: Lilian Lindblom
Illustrations: Anna Koska

Previously published as the *Gifts From Nature: Seasonal Celebrations*

1 3 5 7 9 10 8 6 4 2

ACKNOWLEDGEMENTS
Thanks to the following project contributors:
Fiona Barnett, pp10-11, 20-, 22, 54, 55, 56; Deena Beverley, pp14-15, 30-1, 32, 33, 38-9;
Stephanie Donaldson pp23, 27 34-5, 36-7, 46-7, 50-1; Tessa Evelegh pp12, 42-3, 44, 48, 58, 59, 63;
Joanna Farrow p26, 60; Gilly Love pp13, 16-17; Deborah Schneebeli-Morrell, pp24-5, 45; Liz Wagstaff, pp62p50.
Photographs by: Michelle Garrett, Debbie Patterson, Heini Schneebeli

Contents

Introduction 7

Chapter One

Valentine's Day 8

Chapter Two

Easter 18

Chapter Three

Mother's Day 28

Chapter Four

Harvest and Thanksgiving 40

Chapter Five

Christmas 52

Index 64

Gifts from Nature

Introduction

Traditional festivals punctuate the year in every culture, and have done so throughout history, as successive religions and civilizations simply adopted the celebrations established by older societies. Gathering together and making merry at regular intervals clearly fulfils a very basic human need. But while ancient pagan rites probably included riotous behaviour, modern festive customs are, generally, of an altogether gentler kind: these special times are marked by the exchange of gifts, family parties and convivial meals that invariably include traditional dishes.

The round of the seasons is clearly marked by regular annual festivities, from the symbolic rebirth of nature at Easter to the final gathering-in of the harvest in the autumn. Christmas, the year's most glittering festival, lights up the darkest, coldest days of winter in the northern hemisphere. It is appropriate to draw your inspiration from nature when planning your own celebrations at such times, so that their true spirit and traditions are preserved.

You can bring nature indoors in the shape of fresh flowers in spring and summer, golden corn, nuts and berries in the autumn, and fragrant evergreens for Christmas decorations. Abundant natural materials can form the basis for wonderful gifts. They are rewarding both to make and to receive, and are bound to be in perfect keeping with the time-honoured festivals they mark. These beautiful reflections of the seasons are a refreshing antidote to the high-speed technology and brash commercialism of modern life, which takes all too little account of the gentle but powerful rhythms of the natural world.

Gifts from Nature

Valentine's Day

Romantic gifts and keepsakes are welcome any time, but Valentine's Day, the first festival of the new year, provides the perfect occasion for a little extra pampering of your loved  one. Rich scents and luxurious materials are the order of the day for these tokens of your affection: they will be treasured both for their beauty and for the sentiments they represent, and will be far more  precious to the recipient because they have been specially made by you. Roses are the traditional gift of love, and there are suggestions here for using dried and pressed flowers as well as fresh blooms.

Gifts from Nature

Valentine terracotta pots

Everyone hopes to receive flowers on Valentine's Day and red roses are the traditional choice. These two jewel-like arrangements present them in an original way, contrasting them with acid lime green chrysanthemums in one pot, and combining them richly with purple phlox in the other.

- half block florist's foam
- 2 small terracotta pots, of different sizes
- cellophane (plastic wrap)
- sharp knife
- scissors
- ming fern
- ivy leaves
- 5 stems "Santini" spray chrysanthemums
- 6 stems purple phlox
- 18 dark red roses

1 Soak the florist's foam in water. Line both terracotta pots with cellophane (plastic wrap). Cut the foam into small blocks and wedge the blocks into the lined pots. Trim the cellophane to fit, but do not trim too close to the edges of the pots.

2 Build a dome-shaped foliage outline in proportion to each pot, pushing the stems into the florist's foam. Use ming fern in the larger pot and ivy leaves in the smaller one.

3 In the larger pot, arrange "Santini" chrysanthemums amongst the ming fern. In the smaller pot, distribute the phlox amongst the ivy. In each case, emphasize the domed shape of the arrangement.

4 Strip the leaves from the dark red roses, cut the stems to the desired lengths and arrange them evenly throughout both displays.

Gifts from Nature

Fragrant Drawer Scenter

A deliciously scented cardamom-filled drawer sachet, made from a combination of sumptuous fabrics, makes an original alternative to the traditional lavender bag and is a charming Valentine's gift.

- pencil
- cardboard
- scissors
- scrap of velvet
- 1 m (1 yd) gold-shot organza
- tape measure
- matching sewing thread
- sewing machine
- tacking (basting) thread
- needle
- handful of cardamom pods
- 28 x 15 cm (11 x 6 in) lengths of chenille yarn
- large-eyed needle

1 Draw a freehand heart shape on to cardboard, cut it out and use it to cut a heart from the velvet. Cut four 20 x 15 cm (8 x 6 in) rectangles from the organza. Stitch two rectangles together around all sides, using a straight stitch, to make the front of the sachet. Repeat with the remaining rectangles to make the back. Tack (baste) the heart to the front and appliqué in position. Remove the tacking (basting) thread.

2 With the back and front sections of the sachet right sides together, stitch around three sides. Turn right sides out and fill with cardamom pods. Slip-stitch the remaining side to close. Stitch all around the edge of the sachet, using a zig-zag stitch, and again, 5 mm (¼ in) inside the first line of stitching.

3 Fold one length of chenille yarn in half, thread both ends through a large-eyed needle and pass it through one corner of the sachet. Remove the needle and pull the loop level with the two loose ends. Gather the strands together and tie a knot close to the edge of the sachet. Repeat with the other lengths of chenille to make a fringe of 14 pieces on each side. Trim the ends to an even length.

Gifts from Nature

Rose candles

Plain candles decorated with rose heads and leaves create a stunning, romantic effect. You can also add small metal ornaments or flat beads for extra sparkle, though heavier objects take more practice as speed is crucial if the decoration is to stick before the wax hardens.

- deep, narrow saucepan
- church candles
- pressed rose heads and leaves
- selection of small metal shapes, such as hearts or stars
- flat beads or buttons
- tweezers

1 Fill the saucepan with water, bring it to the boil and remove from the heat. Holding the end of one candle, dip the other end into the water for 4–5 seconds. Remove the candle from the water and immediately stick on as many of the rose heads and decorations as you can before the wax hardens.

2 Repeat the process, turning the candle each time and not leaving it in the water for too long in case the wax melts around the decorations you have already applied. A pair of tweezers may help to push the heavier items into the wax. Repeat for each of the candles.

13

Gifts from Nature

Rose and neroli potpourri

Make this traditional Victorian recipe using the most fragrant petals you can find, perhaps including roses given by your loved one or flowers from a wedding bouquet. Scented with a potent mixture of essential oils and spices, this potpourri will keep for a decade in a closed container.

- 12 fragrant fresh red or pink roses
- paper towels
- glass jar with lid
- 115 g (4 oz/½ cup) sea salt
- tablespoon
- small lid or saucer, to fit inside jar
- wooden spoon
- 15 ml (1 tbsp) whole allspice
- 25 g (1 oz) cinnamon stick
- 5 ml (1 tsp) ground cloves
- pestle and mortar
- sealed container
- 30 ml (2 tbsp) rose water
- 10 drops rose essential oil
- 7 drops rose geranium essential oil
- 7 drops neroli essential oil
- 50 g (2 oz/½ cup) lavender flowers
- 10 ml (2 tsp) ground orris root
- 10 ml (2 tsp) ground mace
- 15 ml (1 tbsp) pink peppercorns
- 5 ml (1 tsp) ground nutmeg
- decorative ceramic container, with lid

1 Remove the rose petals and place on the paper towels, to remove any moisture.

3 Grind the allspice, cinnamon and cloves with the pestle and mortar and reserve half the mixture in a sealed container. Remove the petals from the jar and re-layer with the spices. Replace the lid and set aside for 3 weeks.

2 Place a layer of petals in the glass jar and sprinkle with some of the sea salt. Build up more layers with the remaining petals and salt. Weigh down with a small lid or saucer, then seal the jar. Set aside for 10 days in a cool, dry place, stirring each day with a wooden spoon. Pour off any liquid.

4 Stir in the rose water, essential oils, lavender flowers, remaining spices and reserved spice mix. Set aside for 2 weeks, then transfer to the ceramic container.

The container can be decorated with dried roses, which have first been coated in 15 ml (1 tbsp) sunflower oil scented with 4 drops rose essential oil, and left to steep in a sealed container.

Gifts from Nature

Rose pashka

Surround this creamy confection with extravagant crystallized roses to make an indulgent dessert for a Valentine's dinner. In Russia it is traditionally made in a special wooden mould, but a terracotta flowerpot, well scrubbed and baked in a hot oven for 30 minutes, will do just as well.

- 60 ml (4 tbsp) single (light) cream
- 2 egg yolks
- 75 g (3 oz/⅓ cup) caster (superfine) sugar
- 90 g (3½ oz/scant ½ cup) unsalted butter
- 350 g (12 oz/1½ cups) curd cheese
- 350 g (12 oz/1½ cups) mascarpone cheese
- 10 ml (2 tsp) triple-distilled rose water
- 50 g (2 oz/½ cup) chopped candied peel
- 50 g (2 oz/½ cup) chopped blanched almonds
- crystallized roses, to decorate

For crystallized roses, dip full fresh blooms into beaten egg white to coat evenly, then sprinkle with icing (confectioners') sugar. Leave to dry for about 30 minutes on a wire rack.

1 Heat the cream to just below boiling point. Beat the egg yolks with the sugar until light and add to the cream. Heat together in a saucepan until the mixture thickens, taking care not to let it boil and curdle. Remove the pan from the heat and cool. Beat the butter until creamy and add to the egg and cream mixture. Add the cheeses gradually, then the rose water, candied peel and nuts. Line a flowerpot with muslin and spoon the mixture into it, covering the top with muslin.

2 Weight a small plate on top of the flowerpot and stand it on a plate in the fridge for about 6 hours, or overnight. Turn out the pashka by inverting the flowerpot on to a serving dish and remove the muslin. Decorate the edge of the dish with crystallized roses.

GIFTS FROM NATURE

EASTER

The enduring symbols of the Easter festival are those of nature itself and the beginning of the natural cycle: the bursting buds of new leaves, the energetic growth of spring flowers, the egg with its potential new life. Draw on the youthful freshness and vitality of nature at this time of year for gifts and decorations whose charm and significance far exceed gaudily-wrapped chocolate. Even the most dedicated chocoholics will enjoy decorating real eggs, while apparently bare twigs brought indoors from the garden will blossom magically in the unfamiliar warmth.

GIFTS FROM NATURE

TULIP ARRANGEMENT

The simple beauty of an arrangement which relies entirely on a single type of flower with its own foliage can be breathtaking. This display of soft pink tulips in glorious profusion would make a dramatic Easter table decoration.

- 50 "Angelique" tulips
- small bucket
- basket

1 Strip the lower leaves from the tulips to prevent them from rotting in the water. Fill the bucket with water and place in the basket.

2 Cut each tulip stem to the correct size and place in the water. Arrange the display from its lowest circumference upwards.

3 Continue arranging the tulips towards the centre of the display until a full and even domed shape is achieved. Turn the arrangement to make sure that it can be viewed from all sides.

The arrangement is relatively unstructured but, by repetition of the regular form of the tulip heads, the overall visual effect is that of a dome of flowers to be viewed in the round.

Gifts from Nature

Gerbera Bottle Display

The flowers of the gerbera have a visual innocence and an array of vibrant colours which embody the spirit of Easter. The powerful graphic quality of the gerbera makes it perfect for simple, bold designs.

- red food colouring
- yellow food colouring
- large jug (pitcher)
- 6 slim bottles or vases
- 12 gerberas in various colours
- scissors

1 Add the red and yellow food colourings separately to water and mix thoroughly together. Fill the various bottles or vases. For maximum impact, choose different shapes and sizes of bottles and vary the strength of the food colouring in each.

2 Measure the gerbera stems to the desired height and cut them at an angle. Place them in bottles individually or in twos and threes, depending on the size of the bottle neck. Arrange the bottles in an eye-catching group or display them singly, in a prominent place.

*G*erberas have flexible stems that tend to bend naturally. To straighten them, wrap the top three quarters of the stems in paper and leave to stand in deep cool water for approximately 2 hours.

Decorated Easter Eggs

This is an activity for all the family, and although children may clamour for chocolate eggs, the excitement of dyeing real eggs in different colours and revealing the patterns will keep them involved and entertained.

- hard-boiled eggs
- candle, wax crayon or a piece of beeswax
- natural dyes: turmeric, spinach, onion skins and beetroot (or food colouring)
- small stainless steel saucepans (one for each colour)
- paper towels

1 Draw a freehand pattern on the hard-boiled eggs using a candle, crayon or piece of beeswax.

2 Prepare the dyes and boil the eggs for 5 minutes in each colour.

3 Pat the eggs dry with paper towels. Tuck the decorated eggs into a straw-lined basket.

Natural dyes vary in tone, so experiment to obtain the strength you require. To prepare, boil the food substance in water in a saucepan. The longer it boils, the stronger the colour tone will be.

Gifts from Nature

Bleached spiral eggs

This traditional decorating technique allows very intricate designs to be created on eggshells, using either brushes or dip pens. To start with, try a simple spiral motif in an all-over design. Use only the tiniest amount of bleach, don't let it touch your skin, and work in a well-ventilated space.

- egg drill or skewer
- white hen's or duck's eggs
- pump
- bowl
- natural dye: logwood or walnut shell
- stainless steel saucepan
- slotted spoon
- bleach
- egg cup
- fine paintbrush
- paper towels

1 Using an egg drill, make a hole in the narrow end of an egg, insert the pump and gently pump out the contents. Alternatively, make a small hole in each end of the egg, using a skewer, and blow out the contents. Rinse out the shell under running water.

2 Make up your chosen dye in a saucepan, then add the egg. Ensure that the shell is fully covered and leave it in the dye until it becomes very dark.

3 Pour a little bleach into an egg cup and, using a fine paintbrush, paint spirals on to the egg. Paint dots between the spirals. Leave for about 30 seconds to allow the bleach to eat away at the dyed surface.

4 Wipe away the bleach with a paper towel to reveal the white surface below the dye.

Greek Easter bread

In Greece, Easter celebrations are very important and involve elaborate preparations in the kitchen. This bread, decorated with red dyed eggs, is a traditional part of the Easter feast.

- 25 g (1 oz) fresh yeast
- 120 ml (4 fl oz/½ cup) warm milk
- 675 g (1½ lb/6 cups) plain (all-purpose) flour
- 2 eggs, beaten
- 2.5 ml (½ tsp) caraway seeds
- 15 ml (1 tbsp) caster (superfine) sugar
- 15 ml (1 tbsp) brandy
- 50 g (2 oz/4 tbsp) butter, melted
- 1 egg white, beaten
- 2–3 hard-boiled eggs, dyed with red food colouring
- 50 g (2 oz/½ cup) split almonds

1 Crumble the yeast into a bowl and mix with a little warm water until softened. Add the milk and 115 g (4 oz/1 cup) of the flour and mix to a creamy consistency. Cover with a cloth and leave in a warm place to rise for 1 hour.

2 Sift the remaining flour into a large mixing bowl and make a well in the centre. Pour the risen yeast into the well and draw in a little flour from the sides. Add the eggs, caraway seeds, sugar and brandy. Incorporate the flour to form a dough. Mix in the melted butter. Turn out on to a floured surface and knead for about 10 minutes. Return to the bowl, cover and leave in a warm place for approximately 3 hours.

3 Preheat the oven to 180°C (350°F/Gas 4). Knock back the dough, turn on to a floured surface and knead for a minute or two. Divide the dough into three and roll each piece into a long sausage. Make a plait and place on a greased baking (cookie) sheet. Tuck the ends under, brush with egg white and decorate with the coloured eggs and split almonds. Bake for 1 hour in the oven, until the loaf sounds hollow when tapped on the bottom. Leave to cool on a wire rack.

Gifts from Nature

Simnel Cake

Halfway through Lent it is an old custom to bake a simnel cake, to be brought out to celebrate Easter Day and the end of the lenten fast.

- 225 g (8 oz/2 cups) plain (all-purpose) flour
- pinch of salt
- 115 g (4 oz/⅔ cup) sultanas (golden raisins)
- 50 g (2 oz/½ cup) chopped almonds
- 50 g (2 oz/½ cup) chopped walnuts
- 40 g (1½ oz/3 tbsp) candied peel
- grated rind of ½ lemon
- 75 g (3 oz/3 tbsp) crystallized (candied) ginger, chopped
- 175 g (6 oz/¾ cup) glacé (candied) cherries, quartered
- 200 g (7 oz/scant 1 cup) butter
- 175 g (6 oz/¾ cup) caster (superfine) sugar
- 4 eggs
- 5 ml (1 tsp) vanilla essence (extract)
- 30 ml (2 tbsp) brandy
- apricot jam, sieved, for brushing
- 500 g (1¼ lb) marzipan
- food colouring

1 Preheat the oven to 160°C (325°F/Gas 3). Sift the flour and salt together into a large mixing bowl. Add the sultanas (golden raisins), nuts, candied peel, lemon rind, chopped ginger and cherries and mix, using a wooden spoon. It is important that all the ingredients in the bowl are well coated with the flour.

2 Cream the butter with the sugar until soft. Beat in the eggs one at a time, then add the vanilla essence (extract). Gradually stir in the flour and fruit mixture, adding the brandy with the last of the flour. Pour into a lined 20 cm (8 in) diameter cake tin (pan) and bake for 1 hour. Lower the oven temperature to 150°C (300°F/Gas 2) and bake for another hour.

3 Allow the cake to cool, then store in a tin for 4–6 days before decorating. To decorate the cake, brush the top with sieved apricot jam before rolling out the marzipan and cutting it to fit the cake. Decorate the edge with a marzipan plait and the centre with marzipan eggs, coloured with a little food colouring, if you wish.

Gifts from Nature

Mother's Day

Mothers tend to be the driving force behind most traditional family celebrations, from the initial preparations to the final clearing up. So on Mother's Day it's time to change all that and provide a few welcome surprises for your mother, with treats designed entirely for her enjoyment that will make her feel cherished. A gift you have made yourself will always be specially valued, and never more so than by a doting mother. All these ideas would be very welcome as tokens of your love on other days too – mothers like to feel appreciated all year round.

Gifts from Nature

Wall-Mounted Flowerpot

*Give a garden terracotta flowerpot the antique treatment by painting it in subdued colours, then decorate it with silk rosebuds
and fill with an arrangement of fresh roses for a beautiful gift.*

- terracotta flowerpot
- paintbrush
- matt acrylic paints: dull green, black, white and muddy brown
- glue gun
- silk rosebuds, on wired stems
- pliers
- protective gloves
- wire coathanger
- florist's foam
- fresh roses
- garden moss

1 Working on a protected surface, paint the outside of the terracotta pot with a dry brush, using all the paint colours. Dry brush the inside of the pot with muddy brown paint. Allow the paint to dry completely.

2 Use the glue gun to attach the rosebuds to the sides of the pot in a random, trailing design. Using pliers and wearing protective gloves, untwist the coathanger and make it into a secure loop to suspend the pot.

3 Place florist's dry foam inside the pot. Trim the lower leaves from the stems of the roses, then secure the roses in the foam. Top the surface of the foam with a layer of moss. When the freshness of the flowers eventually fades, the flowerpot will still be in full bloom with a gorgeous display of preserved roses.

Pressed Flower Greeting Card

For a fresh, uncluttered look, restrict your design to a single pressed flower and make the most of its shape. Try turning the flower over to show the undersides of the petals for a change – the soft colours seem appropriate to the ethereal, nostalgic quality of preserved flowers.

- scissors
- watercolour paper
- envelope
- fine paintbrushes
- water-based gold size
- gold leaf or Dutch metal leaf
- PVA (white) glue
- pressed flower
- tweezers

1 Cut the watercolour paper to fit the envelope when folded in half. Using a paintbrush, apply water-based size to selected areas at two opposite corners of the card front. Leave for 20–30 minutes, until clear and tacky, then press the gold or metal leaf on to the size.

2 Using a clean paintbrush, apply glue sparingly to the face of the flower. Pick up the flower with tweezers and gently lay it face down on the card front. Press lightly to secure.

Gifts from Nature

Flower scented ink

Perfumed ink adds a wonderfully romantic touch to letters. For a perfect gift for Mother's Day, add matching scented writing paper. Choose a scent and flowers to suit the colour of the ink, such as lavender oil with violet ink. Strongly coloured inks and strong fragrances are best, as they will both be slightly diluted.

- 25 drops essential oil
- 1 ml (⅛ tsp) vodka
- small ceramic bowl
- funnel
- empty essential oil bottle
- small bottle coloured ink
- copper plant tag
- empty ballpoint pen
- short length of raffia or narrow silk ribbon
- dried or fresh flowers

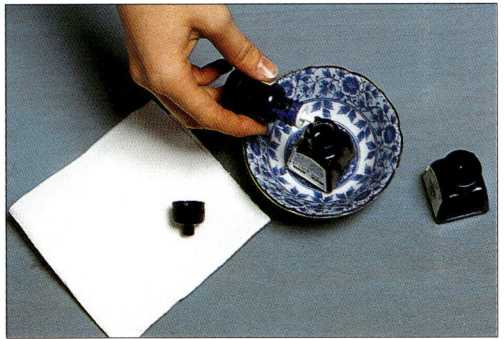

1 Mix the essential oil and vodka in the bowl. Decant into the empty essential oil bottle. Stand the bottle of ink in the bowl and add the oil mixture a drop at a time.

2 Inscribe the name of the scent on the copper tag, using an empty ballpoint pen. Tie the tag around the neck of the ink bottle, using raffia or ribbon, and decorate with flowers.

Gifts from Nature

Luxurious Body Lotions

*Start with a basic, unscented ready-made product, add your own fragrance and use decorative containers to make something luxurious.
These beautifully presented body lotions make wonderful gifts to offer your mother some real pampering pleasure!*

ROSE BODY LOTION

Reminiscent of high summer and romance, rose oil is excellent for all skin types.

- 10 drops rose essential oil
- 175 ml (6 fl oz) unscented body lotion
- decorative bottle
- funnel
- rose leaf
- picture framer's wax guilt
- gold label
- felt-tipped pen

1 Blend the rose essential oil thoroughly into the unscented body lotion.

2 Carefully pour the lotion into a decorative bottle, using a funnel if the neck of the bottle is particularly narrow.

3 For the decoration, gently rub a clean, dry rose leaf with picture framer's wax guilt. Fix the leaf to the bottle and complete the effect by adding a label with a heart motif.

GERANIUM BODY LOTION

A spicily fragrant lotion, geranium oil is derived from a relative of the scented-leaf geranium.

- 10 drops geranium essential oil
- 175 ml (6 fl oz) unscented body lotion
- decorative bottle
- funnel
- geranium leaf
- twine or ribbon
- gold label
- felt-tipped pen

1 Make as for Rose Body Lotion. For the decoration, bind a geranium leaf to the front of the bottle with twine or ribbon. Cut a heart shape from a gold label, write the name of the lotion on it and tie it to the neck of the bottle.

CITRUS BODY LOTION

A refreshing blend of grapefruit and bergamot oils gives this lotion a delightful light fragrance.

- 10 drops grapefruit essential oil
- 10 drops bergamot essential oil
- 175 ml (6 fl oz) unscented body lotion
- decorative bottle
- funnel
- lemon leaf
- twine or ribbon
- gold label
- felt-tipped pen

1 Make as for Rose Body Lotion. For the decoration, bind a lemon leaf to the front of the bottle with twine or ribbon. Write the name of the lotion on the label and attach it to the neck of the bottle.

Citrus oils have a short shelf life and should be used within six months of purchase. As many of them are phototoxic, they should not be applied to the skin before going out in the sun or using a sunbed.

GIFTS FROM NATURE

SCENTED DUSTING POWDER

Dusting powder can be made by blending mica silk, which is a powdered mineral, with cornflour (cornstarch), but mica silk can be difficult to find. A simple solution is to use unscented talcum powder as a base and add essential oils. Rose and jasmine oils are richly perfumed and seductive; peppermint oil is refreshing.

- 75 ml (5 tbsp) talcum powder
- deep mixing bowl
- 15 ml (1 tbsp) cornflour (cornstarch)
- small bowl
- 5 drops rose or jasmine essential oil, or 2 drops peppermint essential oil
- spoon
- decorative lidded container

Pour the talcum powder into a deep bowl. Put the cornflour (cornstarch) in a separate small bowl and add the essential oil. Stir thoroughly to combine. Add the scented flour to the larger bowl and mix. Pour the dusting powder into a decorative lidded container.

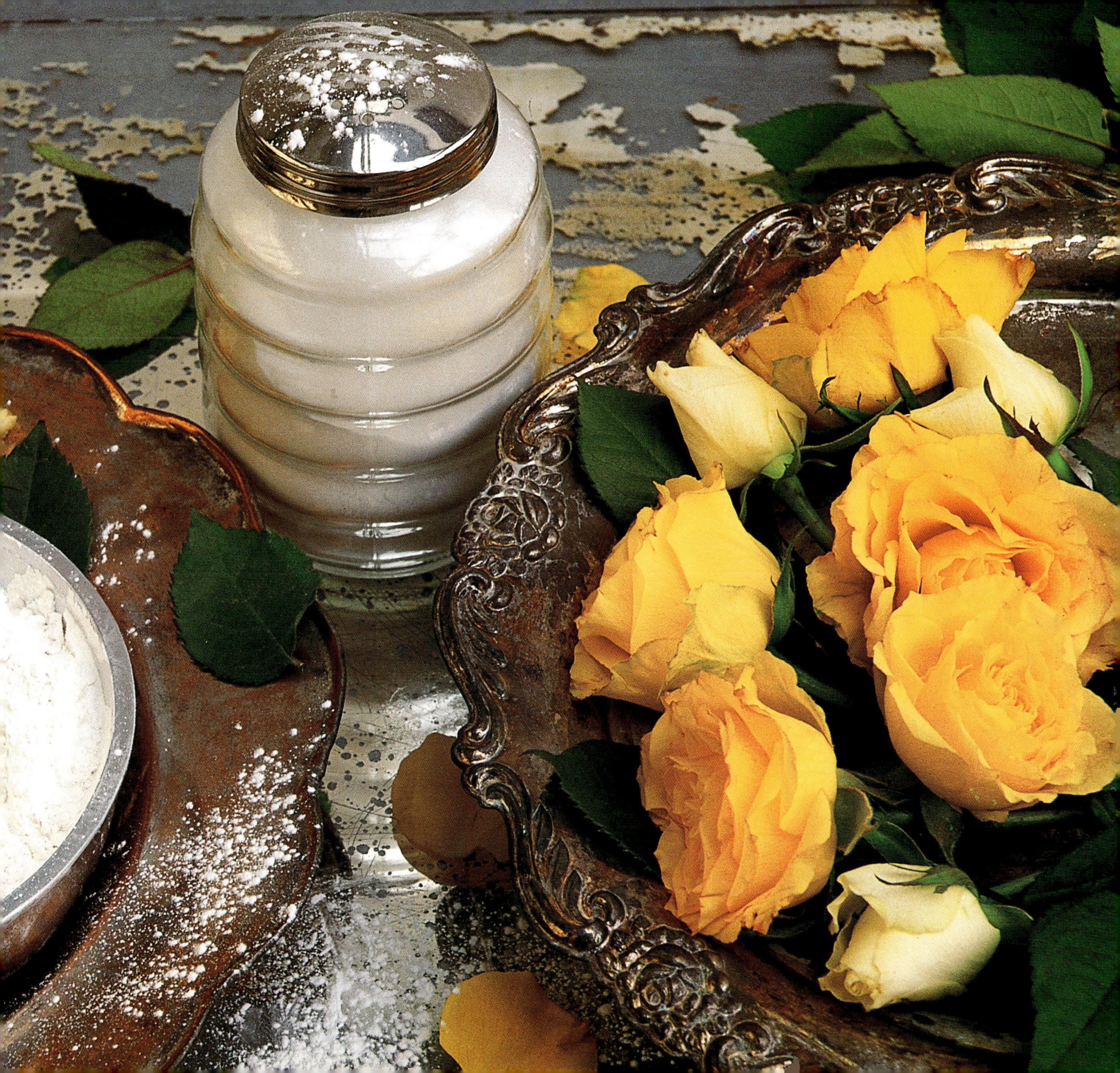

Gifts from Nature

Floral Frosted Orange Cake

Edible flowers make an exquisite decoration for a Mother's Day cake. Dipped individually in orange flower water and sugar, their delicate scent perfectly complements the citrus tang of the cake.

- 225 g (8 oz/1 cup) unsalted (sweet) butter, softened, plus extra for greasing
- 225 g (8 oz/1 cup) caster (superfine) sugar
- 4 large eggs
- 225 g (8 oz/2 cups) self-raising flour
- grated rind of 1 orange

For the frosting:
- 115 g (4 oz/½ cup) unsalted (sweet) butter, softened
- 450 g (1 lb/3½ cups) icing (confectioners') sugar, sifted
- juice of 1 orange

CANDIED FLOWERS

Choose small, pretty, edible flowers such as violets, pansies or primroses. Candied flowers can be made in advance and stored for up to a week between layers of paper towels in an airtight container.

- 300 ml (½ pint/1¼ cups) orange flower water
- small saucepan
- whisk
- 65 g (2½ oz) edible gum arabic
- tweezers
- edible flowers, washed and dried
- 115 g (4 oz/½ cup) caster (superfine) sugar
- paper towels
- wire rack
- airtight container

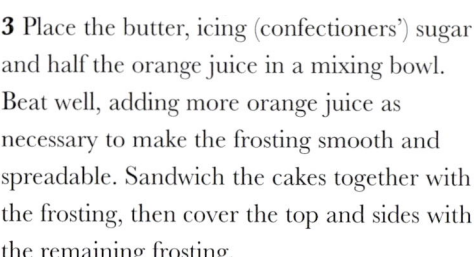

1 Preheat the oven to 190°C (375°F/Gas 5). Place the butter and sugar in a mixing bowl and beat with an electric whisk until very light and fluffy. Add one egg and beat for several minutes. Add the remaining eggs, one at a time, beating well. Sift in the flour all at once, then add the grated orange rind, and mix.

2 Butter and flour two 20 cm (8 in) diameter cake tins (pans), 4 cm (1½ in) deep. Divide the mixture between them. Bake for 30 minutes, or until the cakes spring back when lightly touched in the centre. Cool on a wire rack in the tins for 5 minutes, then turn out the cakes and leave on the rack to cool completely.

3 Place the butter, icing (confectioners') sugar and half the orange juice in a mixing bowl. Beat well, adding more orange juice as necessary to make the frosting smooth and spreadable. Sandwich the cakes together with the frosting, then cover the top and sides with the remaining frosting.

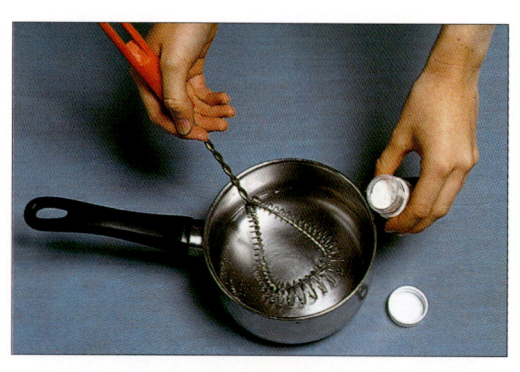

4 For the candied flowers, warm the orange flower water in the saucepan. Whisk in the gum arabic and set aside to cool.

5 Using tweezers, dip each flower in the mixture, shaking to remove the excess. Dip each flower in the sugar, then leave to dry on paper towels on a wire rack for 30 minutes. Decorate the cake with the candied flowers. The flowers may be stored for up to a week in an airtight container lined with paper towels.

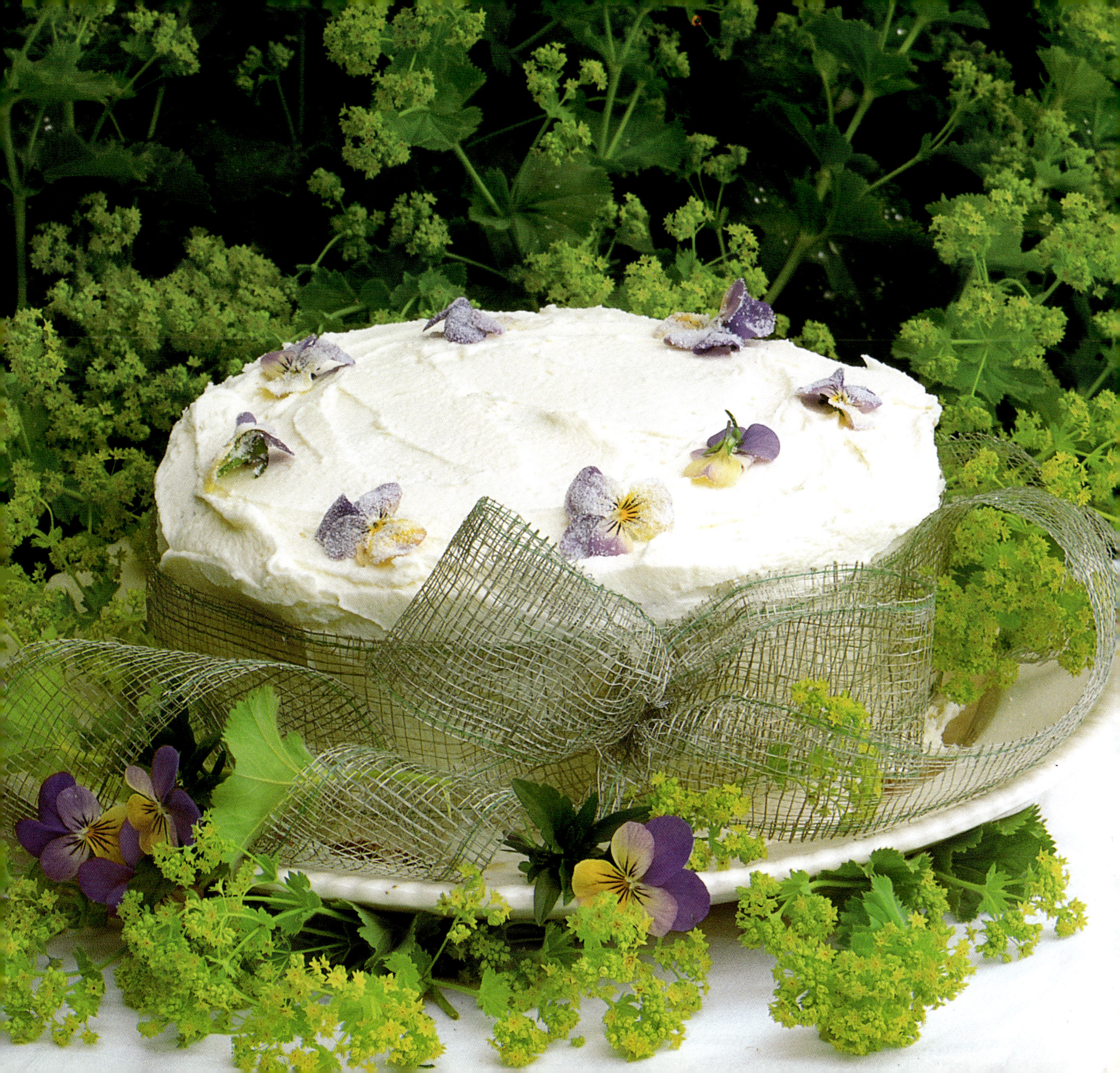

Gifts from Nature

Harvest and Thanksgiving

When foodstore shelves groan all year round with produce flown in from all over the world, it's all too easy to lose sight of harvest time. But autumn is still a time of fruition, when fruits and vegetables from the garden and nuts and berries from the hedgerow make us pause to appreciate the bounty of nature before the dark days of winter. In the New World, Thanksgiving has superceded the traditional Harvest Festival, but many of the symbols of the two festivals are similar. Central to both celebrations is the giving of thanks for the safe gathering-in of the harvest.

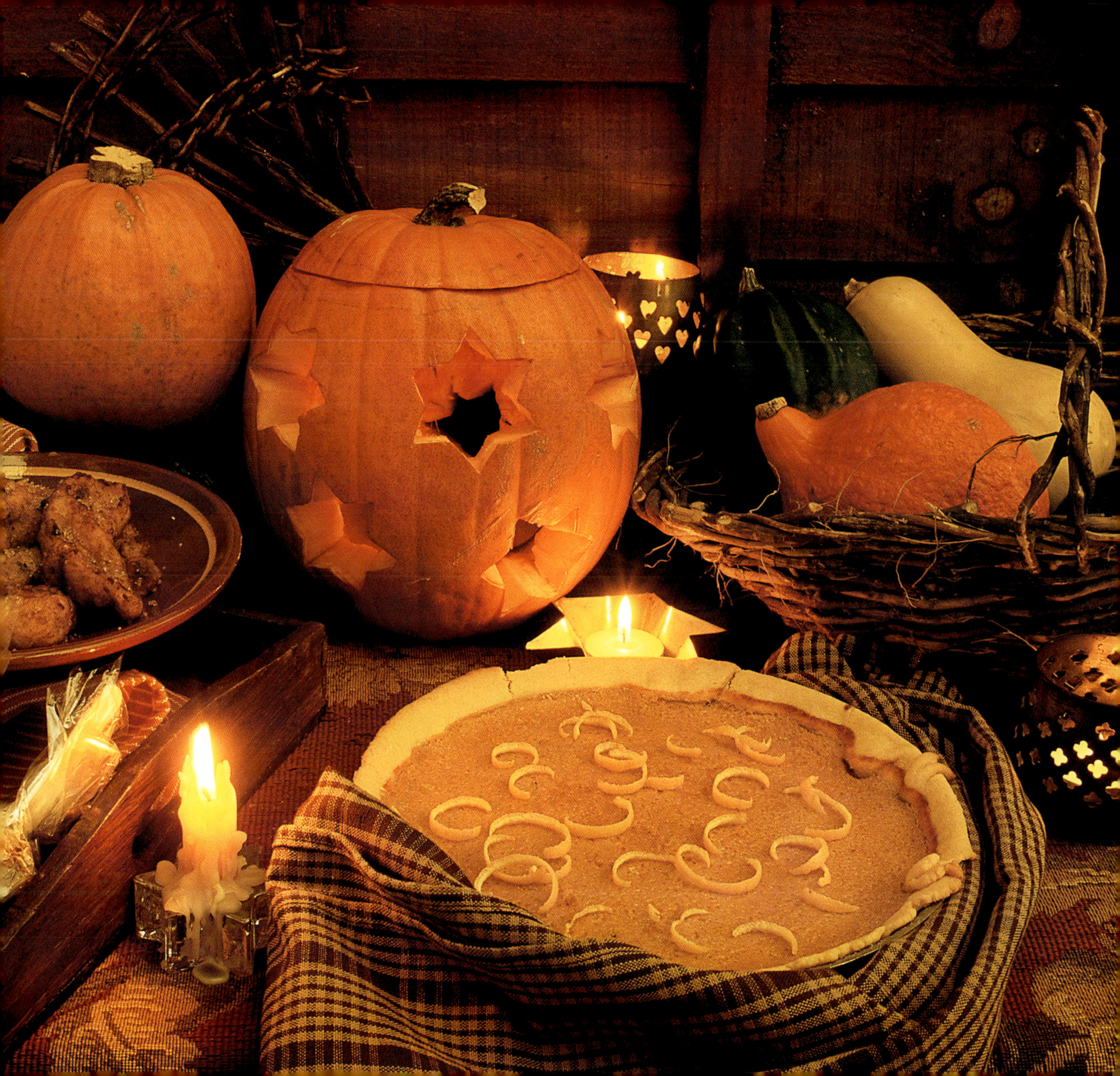

Gifts from Nature

Vegetable Table Decoration

Not all table centres need to include flowers. Here, a still life of ornamental cabbages – complemented by red cabbage and some artichokes – makes a flamboyant focal point. The theme is carried through by adding an ornamental cabbage leaf to each place setting.

- dyed raffia
- wooden basket
- 2 ornamental cabbages in pots
- reindeer moss
- 1 set of cutlery and napkin per person
- small glass jar
- painted garden trug
- red cabbage, halved
- globe artichokes

1 Tie a bow of dyed raffia around the handle of the wooden basket. Remove several perfect cabbage leaves and place the ornamental cabbages, in their pots, in the basket.

2 Cover the tops of the pots with handfuls of reindeer moss.

3 Using raffia, tie up each set of cutlery with a napkin and an ornamental cabbage leaf. Finish the arrangement by putting a few more leaves into a baby food jar and tying dyed raffia around it. Fill a garden trug with the red cabbage halves and the globe artichokes.

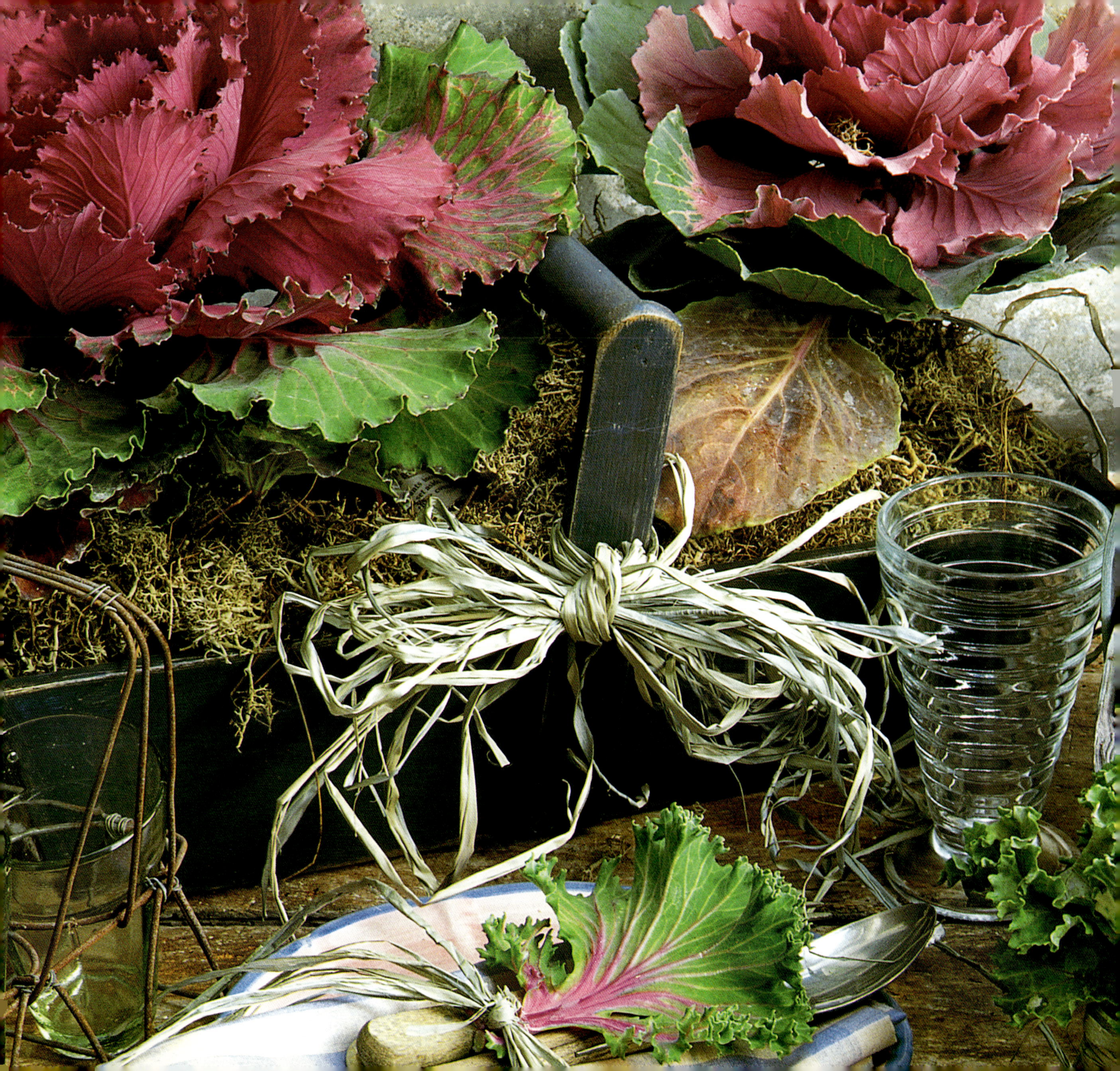

Gifts from Nature

Autumn Gold

The gold tints of autumn can be gathered into a fabulous display, using even the humblest of containers. Here, dahlias have been simply arranged in a preserving jar and given a seasonal necklace of hazelnuts.

- hazelnuts
- seagrass string
- secateurs (pruning shears)
- 12 dahlia stems
- preserving jar
- small pumpkins
- branches of pyracantha with berries

1 Tie the hazelnuts on to the seagrass string to make a necklace.

2 Cut about 1 cm (½ in) off the end of each dahlia stem and place the flowers in the preserving jar filled with water.

3 Tie the hazelnut necklace around the jar. Finish the arrangement with small pumpkins and pyracantha branches.

44

Gifts from Nature

Pale Beauty

An elegant squash in palest green has an almost luminous quality about it and needs only a few carved holes to transform it into a captivating autumn light. Remember that burning candles should never be left unattended.

- water-soluble crayon
- pale green squash
- sharp knife
- woodcarving tool
- 2.5 cm (1 in) diameter drill bit
- short candle

1 Using the crayon, draw a circle on the top of the squash about 8 cm (3½ in) in diameter. Cut around the circle, then scoop out the seeds with your hands. Using the woodcarving tool, chip and carve away at the solid orange flesh until the shell is no more than 2 cm (¾ in) thick.

2 Holding the drill bit in your hand, pierce through the shell using a pushing and twisting action. Once it is through, remove it by twisting it back in an anticlockwise direction so you do not damage the skin around the hole. Repeat in a random design all over the shell. Insert the candle.

45

Gifts from Nature

Decorative wheat

In pagan times, a miniature stook of wheat would have been erected in the home as an offering to the gods; it still makes an attractive country-style decoration. You can buy bunches of wheat from a dried flower supplier.

CONTAINER DISPLAY

Using a flat-backed container means the display can be left free-standing or attached to a wall.

- 4 bunches of wheat
- garden wire or string
- flat-backed tin container
- natural raffia

Undo the bunches of wheat and adjust the heads so that they are level. Bind the bunches together at the bottom and arrange in the tin container. Decorate with a raffia bow.

HARVEST WHEATSHEAF

This traditional arrangement would look just as good indoors or out.

- 4 bunches of wheat
- garden wire or string
- silver birch twigs

Prepare three bunches of wheat as for the Container Display, then tie them together in one large bunch. Use the remaining wheat as the outer layer of the wheatsheaf and tie it in place. Trim the bases of the stems level. Twist the silver birch twigs into and around the wheatsheaf and tie them securely in place.

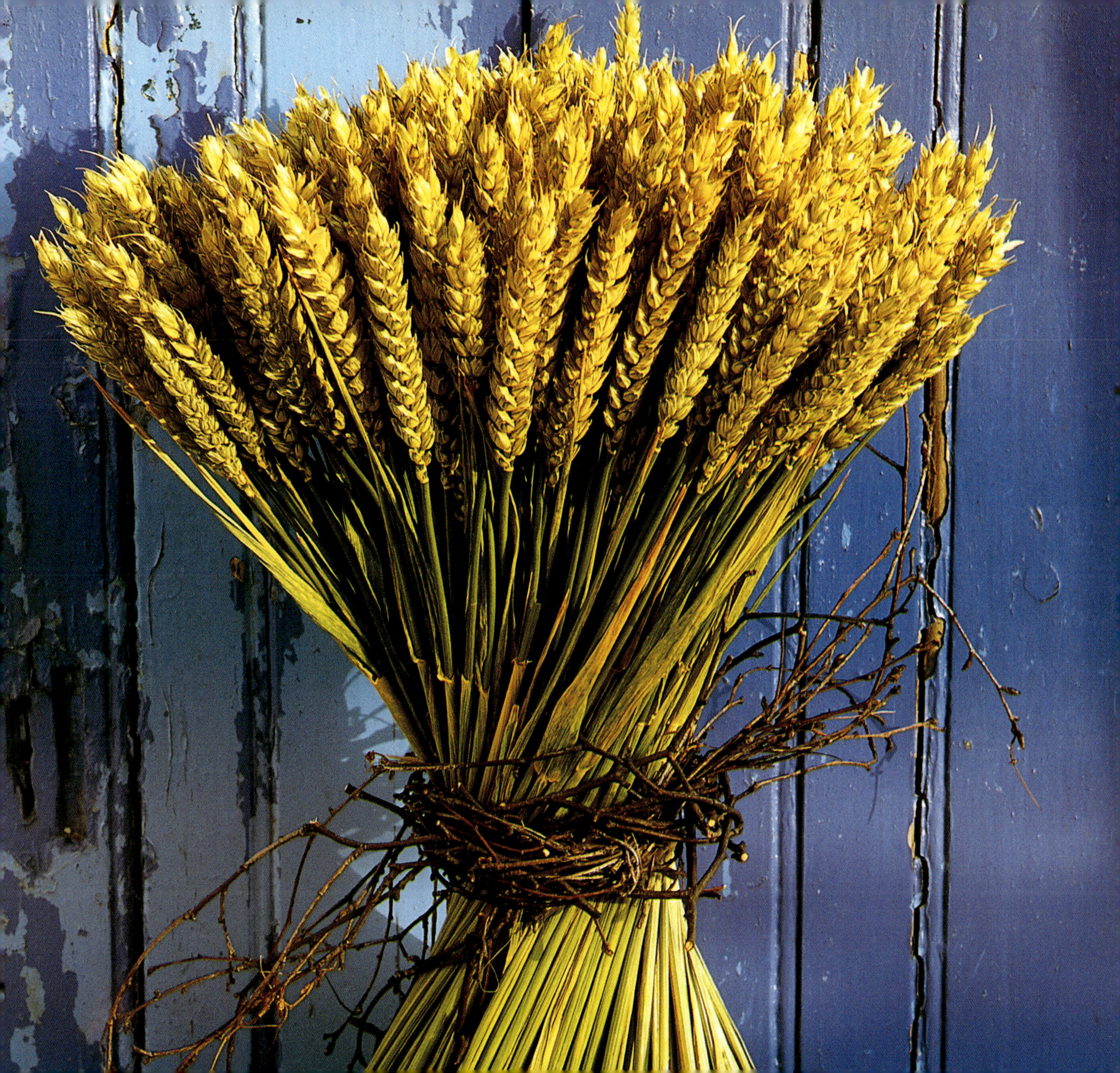

Gifts from Nature

Spiced Pickled Pears

These pears, spiced with cardamom, are delicious with cold roast meats and salad. This quantity will fill three medium-size preserving jars, but if you have a glut of pears, home-made preserves like this make lovely gifts.

- 30 ml (2 tbsp) lemon juice
- 2 kg (5 lb) pears
- 750 ml (1¼ pints/3 cups) red wine vinegar
- 1 kg (2¼ lb/5 cups) sugar
- 10 ml (2 tsp) cardamom pods
- 10 ml (2 tsp) black peppercorns
- 3 bay leaves
- 3 strips orange rind

1 Half-fill a large saucepan or preserving pan with cold water and add the lemon juice. Discard the pear stalks, then peel and halve the pears and cut out the cores. Immediately place the pears in the pan.

2 Bring the water to the boil and cook the pears for 15 minutes, or until tender. Drain in a colander. Pour the vinegar into the pan and add the sugar. Split the cardamom pods, roughly crush the peppercorns and add the spices to the vinegar with the bay leaves and orange rind. Bring to the boil and simmer until the sugar has dissolved. Return the pears to the pan and leave to simmer for 10 minutes, turning the fruit several times so that it cooks evenly.

3 Lift the pears out with a slotted spoon and pack into warm, dry, sterilized jars. Strain the vinegar into the jars, making sure the pears are well covered. Add the bay leaves and orange rind and wedge the fruit below the surface of the vinegar with some crumpled greaseproof paper. Seal well and leave to cool. Allow to mature for at least 2 weeks before eating. The pears will keep for up to 3 months in a cool, dark place. Once opened, they should be stored in the fridge.

GIFTS FROM NATURE

PUMPKIN PIE

While the children cut grinning faces in their pumpkin shells and line them up on the windowsill for Halloween, you can transform the flesh into this luxurious, spicy pumpkin pie.

- 450 g (1 lb) pumpkin
- 175 g (6 oz/¾ cup) brown sugar
- 175 ml (6 fl oz/¾ cup) milk
- 4 eggs
- 250 ml (8 fl oz/1 cup) double (heavy) cream
- 50 ml (2 fl oz/¼ cup) brandy
- 10 ml (2 tsp) ground cinnamon
- 2.5 ml (½ tsp) ground ginger or grated nutmeg
- 2.5 ml (½ tsp) salt
- 25 cm (10 in) flan tin (pan) lined with shortcrust pastry, chilled

1 Chop the pumpkin flesh into small cubes.

2 Steam the cubed pumpkin until soft, for about 10–15 minutes, and leave to drain, preferably overnight.

3 Preheat the oven to 180°C (350°F/Gas 4). Place the cooled, drained pumpkin in a food processor with all the remaining filling ingredients and blend to a smooth texture. Pour into the prepared pastry case and bake in the preheated oven for 1¼ hours.

Gifts from Nature

Harvest loaf

The harvest loaf is the centrepiece of the traditional Harvest Festival, displayed on the church altar amongst the fruit and vegetables and other offerings. Although there are many different designs, the most enduringly popular is the wheatsheaf.

- 750 g (1¾ lb/ 7 cups) strong white flour,
- 15 ml (1 tbsp) salt
- 10 g (¼ oz) dried yeast
- sugar, to activate yeast
- beaten egg, to glaze

1 Sift the flour and salt into a bowl and make a well. Mix the yeast with 60 ml (4 tbsp) warm water and a little sugar and leave for about 15 minutes. Add the yeast mixture and 350 ml (12 fl oz/1½ cups) water to the flour and mix, using your hands. Turn out on to a floured surface and knead until the dough becomes elastic. Place in an oiled bowl, cover and leave for 2 hours, until the dough has doubled in size.

3 Divide the remaining dough in half, then divide one half in two again. Use one half to make the stalks of the wheat by rolling into narrow ropes and placing on the "stalk" of the sheaf. Use the other half of the dough to make a plait to decorate the finished loaf where the stalks meet the ears of wheat.

2 Preheat the oven to 220°C (425°F/Gas 7). Roll 225 g (8 oz) of the dough into a 30 cm (12 in) long cylinder. Place the cylinder on an oiled, floured baking (cookie) sheet and flatten it with your hand. This will form the base for the long stalks of the wheatsheaf. Take 350 g (12 oz) of the remaining dough, roll and shape it into a crescent. Place this at the top of the cylinder and flatten it with your hand.

4 For the ears of wheat, roll out sausage shapes from the remaining dough and snip with scissors to give the effect of the ears. Place on the crescent, fanning them out from the base until the wheatsheaf is complete. Position the plait between the stalks and the ears of wheat. Brush the wheatsheaf with the egg. Bake for 20 minutes, then reduce the heat to 160°C (325°F/Gas 3) and bake for 20 minutes more.

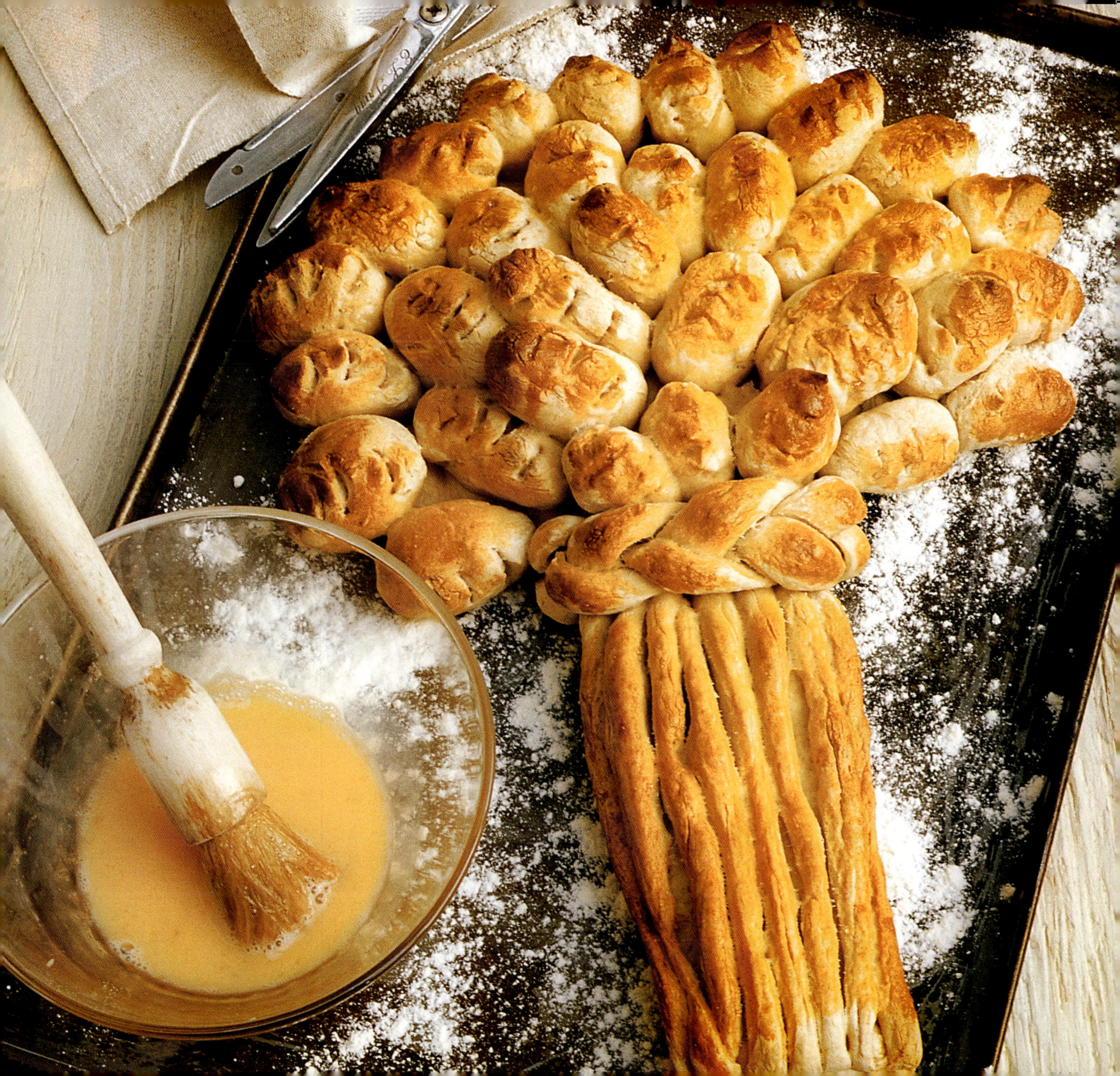

GIFTS FROM NATURE

CHRISTMAS

During the biggest seasonal celebration of the year, the commercialization and glitz can easily become oppressive. Redress the balance and restore a sense of calm by leaving the tinsel in its box and decorating your home with beautiful evergreen foliage and natural materials such as cones, berries, dried fruits and flowers. Instead of toiling through the crowds to buy gifts, time spent at home making delicious and beautiful things can be both rewarding and fun: you'll be inspired with the true spirit of Christmas, and your friends and family will love their original and unique presents.

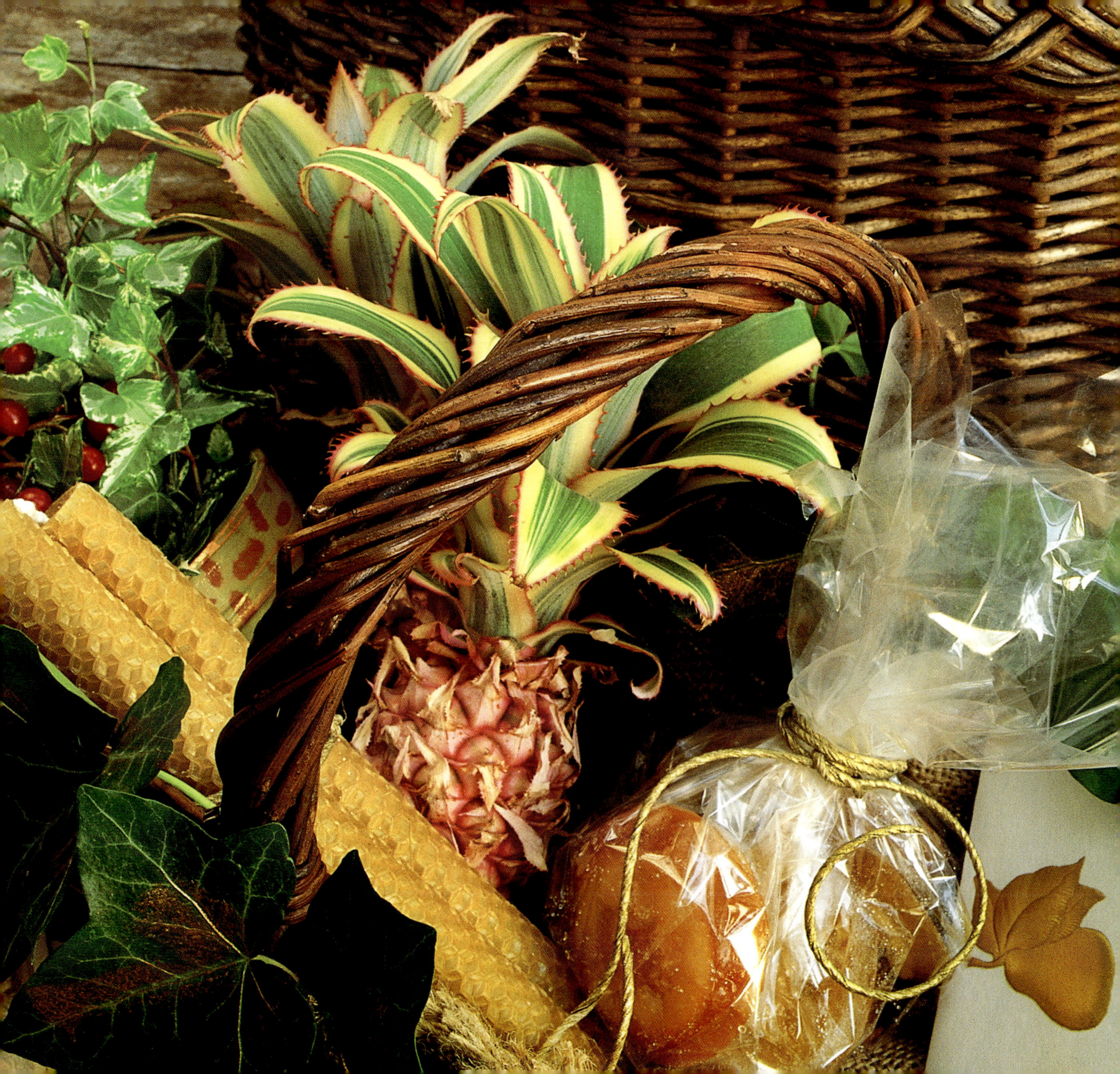

Gifts from Nature

Mistletoe Kissing Ring

Instead of just tying a bunch of mistletoe to some strategically placed light-fitting in the hall, make a traditional kissing ring that can be hung up as a Christmas decoration and still serve as a focal point for a seasonal kiss!

- scissors
- 7 winterberry stems
- large bunch of mistletoe
- garden twine
- 1 twisted cane ring
- 2.5 m (2¾ yd) tartan (plaid) ribbon

1 Cut the stems of the winterberry into 18 cm (7 in) lengths. Divide the mistletoe into 14 substantial stems and use twine to tie the smaller sprigs into bunches. Attach a branch of winterberry to the outside of the ring with the twine. Add a stem, or bunch, of mistletoe so that it overlaps about one-third of the length of winterberry, and bind in place. Bind on another stem of winterberry, overlapping the mistletoe.

2 Repeat the sequence until the outside of the cane ring is covered in a "herringbone" pattern of materials. Cut the ribbon into 4 equal lengths. Tie one end of each piece of ribbon to the decorated ring at four equidistant points around its circumference. Bring the four ends of the ribbon up above the ring and tie into a bow; this will enable you to suspend the finished kissing ring.

54

Advent Candle Wreath

An Advent candle wreath has four candles, one to be lit on each of the four Sundays leading up to Christmas Day. This one is built on a pine foliage ring and uses fruits and spices for its decoration.

- 30 cm (12 in) blue pine foliage ring
- 4 x 30 cm (12 in) candles
- scissors
- glue gun and glue sticks
- 12 slices dried orange
- 16 short cinnamon sticks
- 4 fresh clementines
- 6 dried cut lemons
- 5 dried whole oranges
- 4 fir cones
- 4 physalis heads
- ribbon
- florist's wire

1 Attach the four candles at equal distances around the ring by cutting away some of the pine needles, putting hot glue on both the base of the candle and on the ring and pressing the two surfaces together for a few seconds. At the base of each candle, glue an arrangement of the orange slices and cinnamon sticks.

2 Make sure each candle has an interesting selection of the materials at its base. Make four bows from the ribbon and bind with florist's wire at their centres. Attach these to the wreath by pulling the tails of wire around the width of the ring, twisting together and returning the cut ends into the moss.

3 Position one bow at each of the four central points between the candles. Make sure that the bows do not touch the candles and remember that burning candles should never be left unattended.

Gifts from Nature

Christmas tree decorations

These charming tree ornaments use dried flower-arranging materials, supplemented with some gold dust powder and gold cord. They are extremely easy to make.

For the stars and Christmas trees:
- 1 block florist's dry foam
- sharp knife
- shaped pastry cutters
- loose dried lavender
- gold dust powder
- plastic bag
- florist's adhesive
- dried tulip and rose petals
- cranberries
- gold cord
- scissors

For the dried fruit decorations:
- gold cord
- dried oranges and limes
- florist's adhesive
- dried red and yellow rose heads
- cinnamon sticks
- needle

1 To make the stars and Christmas trees, cut the block of florist's dry foam into slices about 2.5 cm (1 in) thick. Using the pastry cutters, cut star and tree shapes from the foam. Mix the lavender with the gold dust powder in a plastic bag (first making sure the bag has no holes in it) and shake together. Liberally coat all the surfaces of the foam shapes with florist's adhesive.

2 Place the adhesive-covered shapes, one at a time, in the bag of lavender and gold dust powder, and shake. The shape will be coated with the lavender heads and powder. As a variation, press some dried tulip and rose petals on to the glued shapes before putting them into the bag – only the exposed glued areas will pick up the lavender. As a further variation, glue a cranberry to the centre of some of the stars. Use a needle to make a hole in each shape. Thread a piece of cord through the hole and make a loop for hanging the decoration from the Christmas tree.

3 To make the dried fruit decorations, first tie the gold cord around the fruit, crossing it over at the bottom and knotting it at the top to make a hanging loop. Dab a blob of florist's adhesive on to the base of a rose head and stick it to the fruit next to the knotted gold cord at the top. Dab some adhesive on to two or three short pieces of cinnamon stick and glue these on to the dried fruit, grouping them with the rose head.

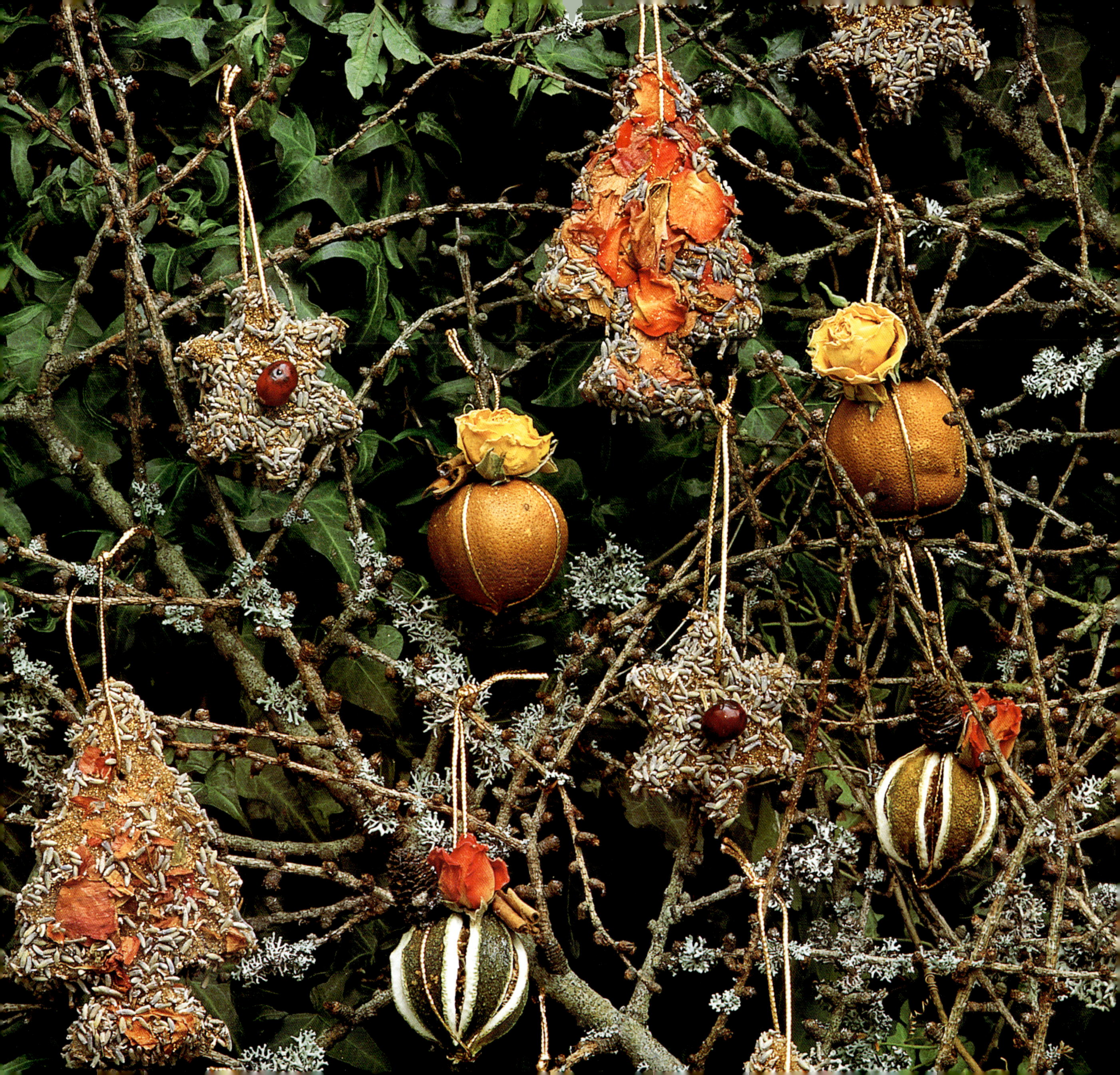

Gifts from Nature

Starry spice giftwrap

Gold tissue, clear cellophane (plastic wrap) and gilded star anise make for an extremely elegant giftwrap, which can be used for the most awkwardly shaped gifts. Tissue takes easily to any form and the transparent wrap allows space for curves, corners and points.

- gold tissue paper
- cellophane (plastic wrap)
- gold cord
- picture framer's gilt wax
- star anise
- glue gun

1 Wrap the gift in gold tissue. This bottle has a cracker-style end; a square or rectangular parcel could be completely wrapped in the normal way.

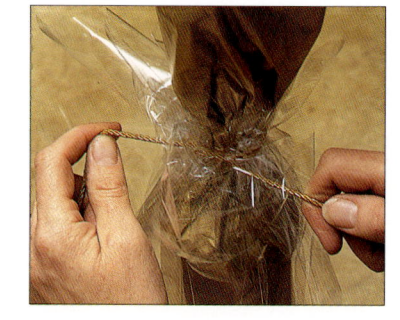

2 Cut enough cellophane (plastic wrap) to over-wrap the parcel loosely and tie it at the top with a length of gold cord.

3 Gently rub picture framer's gilt wax on to the star anise with your index finger.

4 Using the glue gun, fix the star anise in position on the wrap, placing them at regular intervals.

Gifts from Nature

Christmas Gift Basket

Decorate a willow basket with gilded ivy leaves, then pack it with seasonal goodies: a pot of variegated ivy and berries, decorative florist's pineapples, and treats such as beeswax candles and crystallized (candied) fruits.

- tree ivy
- picture framer's gilt wax
- willow basket
- scissors
- hessian (burlap)
- pot of variegated ivy with berries
- seasonal presents

1 Gild the tree ivy by rubbing on picture framer's gilt wax, using your fingers. Decorate the rim of the basket with these gilded leaves.

2 Cut a piece of hessian (burlap) to size and fray the edges. Use the hessian to line the basket. Add the pot of ivy and seasonal gifts to fill the basket.

59

Gifts from Nature

Chocolate Fruit and Nut Cookies

These chunky Lebkuchen cookies make a delicious gift, especially when presented in a decorative box.

For the Lebkuchen:
- 4 oz (8 tbsp/1 stick) unsalted (sweet) butter, softened
- 4 oz (100 g/½ cup) brown sugar
- 1 egg, beaten
- 13 oz (1 cup) molasses
- 12 oz (3 cups) self-raising flour
- 1 tsp ground ginger
- ½ tsp ground cloves
- ¼ tsp chilli powder

For the decoration:
- 50 g (2 oz/¼ cup) caster (superfine) sugar
- 75 ml (5 tbsp) water
- 225 g (8 oz) plain (semisweet) chocolate
- 50 g (2 oz/¼ cup) walnut halves
- 175 g (6 oz/¾ cup) glacé (candied) cherries, cut into wedges
- 115 g (4 oz/1 cup) whole blanched almonds

1 Cream together the butter and sugar in a bowl until pale and fluffy. Beat in the egg and molasses, then sift in the flour, ginger, cloves and chilli powder. Using a wooden spoon, combine the ingredients to make a stiff paste. Turn out onto a floured surface and knead until smooth. Wrap and chill for 30 minutes.

2 Preheat the oven to 180°C (350°F/Gas 4). Grease two baking (cookie) sheets. Shape the dough into a roll 20 cm (8 in) long and chill for 30 minutes. Cut into 20 slices and space them on the sheets. Bake for 10 minutes. Leave to cool for 5 minutes before transferring the slices to a wire rack to cool completely.

3 Put the sugar in a small, heavy saucepan with the water. Heat until the sugar dissolves. Bring to the boil and boil for 1 minute, until slightly syrupy. Leave to cool slightly, then stir in the chocolate, broken up, until melted.

4 Spoon a little of the chocolate mixture over each cookie, spreading it to the edges with the back of the spoon.

5 Gently press a walnut half into the centre of each cookie. Arrange pieces of glacé (candied) cherry and almonds alternately around the walnuts and leave to set.

GIFTS FROM NATURE

GILDED NUTS

Nuts are ideal subjects for gilding as they have so much texture and detail. They would make a sumptuous Christmas table decoration, and look lovely wired on to evergreen garlands, or used as the finishing touches to opulent giftwraps.

- assorted nuts
- red oxide spray primer
- medium paintbrushes
- water-based gold size
- gold Dutch metal leaf
- burnishing brush or soft cloth
- amber shellac varnish

1 Spray the nuts with red oxide spray primer and leave to dry.

2 Paint on a thin, even coat of water-based size and leave for 20–30 minutes, until it becomes clear and tacky.

3 Wrap the sized nuts in sheets of gold Dutch metal leaf, making sure that they are completely covered and that no recesses or details are exposed.

4 Burnish the nuts with a burnishing brush or soft cloth to remove the excess leaf. Seal with a thin, even coat of amber shellac varnish and leave to dry.

Gifts from Nature

Gingered Hot Toddy

This spicy drink is not only delicious and warming, it can relieve the early symptoms of influenza if taken at bedtime. Make a gift presentation of the ingredients and include the recipe, so the recipient knows how to put the drink together.

- scissors
- gold organza
- jar of stem (preserved) ginger
- jar of clear honey
- gold ribbon
- bottle of whisky
- miniature decanter
- lemon
- decorative wire basket
- label
- felt-tipped pen

1 Cut two pieces of gold organza to fit over the lids of the jars. Tie with lengths of gold ribbon.

2 Pour the whisky into a miniature decanter, and arrange all the ingredients for the toddy in the basket.

3 On a decorative label, write the following recipe: "Finely slice one piece of stem (preserved) ginger and put it in a heatproof glass with 10 ml (2 tsp) honey and a slice of lemon. Two-thirds fill with boiling water, add whisky and stir in lemon juice to taste. Sip while piping hot for a warming, therapeutic effect just before you drift off."

Index

Advent candle wreath, 55
Autumn gold, 44

Bleached spiral eggs, 24–5
Body lotions, luxurious, 34–5
Bread
  Greek Easter bread, 26
  harvest loaf, 50–1

Cakes
  floral frosted orange cake, 38–9
  simnel cake, 27
Candied flowers, 16, 38
Candles
  Advent candle wreath, 55
  rose candles, 13
Chocolate fruit and nut cookies, 60–1
Christmas, 52–63
  Christmas gift basket, 59
  Christmas tree decorations, 56–7
Cookies, chocolate fruit and nut, 60–1

Decorated Easter eggs, 23
Decorative wheat, 46–7
Dusting powder, scented, 36–7

Easter, 18–27
Eggs
  bleached spiral eggs, 24–5
  decorated Easter eggs, 23

Floral frosted orange cake, 38–9
Flower scented ink, 33
Fragrant drawer scenter, 12

Gerbera bottle display, 22
Giftwrap, starry spice, 58
Gilded nuts, 62
Gingered hot toddy, 63
Greek Easter bread, 26
Greeting card, pressed flower, 32

Harvest Festival, 40–51
Harvest loaf, 50–1

Ink, flower scented, 33

Luxurious body lotions, 34–5

Mistletoe kissing ring, 54
Mother's Day, 28–39

Nuts, gilded, 62

Pale beauty, 45
Pashka, rose, 16–17
Pears, spiced pickled, 48

Potpourri, rose and neroli, 14–15
Pressed flower greeting card, 32
Pumpkin pie, 49

Roses
  Advent candle wreath, 55
  rose candles, 13
  rose and neroli potpourri, 14–15
  rose pashka, 16–17
  Valentine terracotta pots, 10–11

Scented dusting powder, 36–7
Simnel cake, 27
Spiced pickled pears, 48
Squash, pale beauty, 45
Starry spice giftwrap, 58

Thanksgiving, 40–51
Toddy, gingered hot, 63
Tulip arrangement, 20–1

Valentine's Day, 8–17
Valentine terracotta pots, 10–11
Vegetable table decoration, 42–3

Wall-mounted flowerpot, 30–1
Wheat, decorative, 46–7